The *bloomer* is as notorious as a spoonerism. It is a horrible *double entendre* committed in all innocence (as when Henry James unwittingly wrote, 'She realised at last that she had no vocation for struggling with her combinations'). Henry James is well represented in this brazen, hilarious collection presented without a blush. Heath provides some contemporary illustrations to the unintentional statements of a wide range of writers.

illustrated by HEATH

London
UNWIN PAPERBACKS
Boston   Sydney

First published by The Bodley Head as
An Adult's Garden of Bloomers 1966
and *A New Garden of Bloomers* 1967

This collection with illustrations first published in
Unwin Paperbacks 1982

UNWIN® PAPERBACKS
40 Museum Street, London WC1A 1LU, UK

Unwin Paperbacks
Park Lane, Hemel Hempstead, Herts

George Allen & Unwin Australia Pty Ltd,
8 Napier Street, North Sydney, NSW 2060, Australia

British Library Cataloguing in Publication Data

Bloomers.
1. English wit and humor
I. Heath II. A New garden of bloomers III. An
Adult's garden of bloomers
828'.08   PN6151
ISBN 0-04-827058-X

Set in Souvenir by Fotographics (Bedford) Ltd
and printed in Great Britain by
Richard Clay (The Chaucer Press) Ltd, Bungay, Suffolk

Grateful acknowledgement is made to the following copyright-holders for permission to reprint quotations from the authors listed:

Edward Arnold Ltd (E. M. Forster: *A Room with a View*)

Ernest Benn Ltd (A. M. W. Stirling)

Blandford Press Ltd (R. W. Harris)

Geoffrey Bles Ltd (C. S. Lewis)

Chatto & Windus Ltd and Mr George Scott Moncrieff (Marcel Proust: *Cities of the Plain*)

Constable & Co Ltd and the Estate of the late Patrick Hamilton (Patrick Hamilton)

J. M. Dent & Sons Ltd and the Trustees of the Joseph Conrad Estate (Joseph Conrad and Jerome K. Jerome)

Hamish Hamilton Ltd (Angela Thirkell: *The Brandons*)

David Higham Associates Ltd and Victor Gollancz Ltd (Dorothy L. Sayers)

Longmans, Green & Co (Dame Ethel Smyth)

Macmillan & Co Ltd London, and The Macmillan Company of Canada Ltd (Thomas Hardy: *Under the Greenwood Tree* and *The Woodlanders*)

A. D. Peters as the literary representatives of the Estate of the late Rose Macaulay (Rose Macaulay: *Personal Pleasures*)

Laurence Pollinger Ltd and Frederick Warne Ltd (Frances Hodgson Burnett)

Sidgwick & Jackson Ltd (E. M. Forster: *The Story of a Panic*)

The Society of Authors as the literary representative of the Estate of the late A. E. Housman, and Messrs Jonathan

Jerome K. Jerome

The only thing I can think about now is
being hard up. I suppose having my hands
in my pockets has made me think about
this. I always do sit with my hands in my
pockets, except when I am in the company
of my sisters, my cousins, or my aunts; and
they kick up such a shindy – I should say
expostulate so eloquently on the subject
– that I have to give up and take them out
– my hands I mean.

Idle Thoughts of an Idle Fellow

BLOOMERS

Anon

Meredith had an unbounded enthusiasm for French letters. 'He lost his sense of proportion in that matter,' said Henry James to Alice Meynell.

Nonesuch edition of Meredith's letters to Alice Meynell

Charles Reade

And when you had found him, you found a
man superficially coy perhaps, but at
bottom always ready to do business.

It's Never Too Late to Mend

Horace Annesley Vachell

He reached his room to find three other
boys busily engaged in abusing their
housemaster. They took no notice of John,
who leaned against the wall.

The Hill

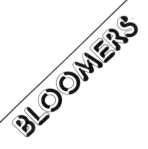

Anthony Trollope

She gave a little scream and a jerk, and so relieved herself . . .

The Duke's Children

Mrs Ray declared that she had not found it all hard and then – with a laudable curiosity, seeing how little she had known about balls – desired to have an immediate account of Rachel's doings.

Rachel Ray

Mrs Gaskell

I've a great respect for Miss Tomkinson; but I do assure you, sir, I'd as soon marry one of Her Majesty's Life Guards. I would rather; it would be more suitable.

Mr Harrison's Confessions

William Hazlitt

P.S. I like my balls very well, and have also received the money.

From a letter to his mother, written at the age of 12

BLOOMERS

BLOOMERS

H. Bonar

Soon shalt thou hear the Bridegroom's
voice,
 The midnight cry, 'Behold, I come!'

Public School Hymn Book No. 304

BLOOMERS

Somerset Maugham

Mind you, I never made advances to a woman who wouldn't have gladly acknowledged to thirty-five. And I give them love. Why, many of them had never known what it was to have a man do them up behind.

The Round Dozen

A. W. Stirling

Mrs Haywood's father was Edward
Corbould, a celebrated artist in his day,
who was intimate with all the Royal
Family.

Victorian Sidelights

Charlotte Brontë

He flourished his tool. The end of the lash
just touched my forehead. A warm excited
thrill ran through my veins, my blood
seemed to give a bound, and then raced
fast and hot along its channels. I got up
nimbly, came round to where he stood, and
faced him.

The Professor

BLOOMERS

Jane Austen

Mrs Goddard was the mistress of a School
– not of a seminary, or an establishment, or
any thing which professed, in long
sentences of refined nonsense, to combine
liberal acquirements with elegant
morality upon new principles and new
systems – and where young ladies for
enormous pay might be screwed out of
health and into vanity . . .

Emma

Such was Catherine Morland at ten. At
fifteen appearances were mending; she
began to cut her hair and long for balls . . .

Northanger Abbey

Author of
Little Dot, My Mates and I,
Saved at Sea etc

Poor old Treffy was in bad spirits this evening. He felt that he and his organ were getting out of date, things of the past. They were growing old together. He could remember the day when it was new. How proud he had been of it! Oh, he had admired it . . . But when he had eaten his cake and had taken some tea which he had warmed over again, old Treffy felt rather better, and he turned as usual to his old organ to cheer his fainting spirits. For old Treffy knew nothing of a better comforter. The landlady of the house had objected at first to old Treffy's organ; she said it disturbed the lodgers.

Christie's Old Organ

'Yes,' said little Mabel; 'I wish I had an organ, don't you, Charlie?'
'Shall I ask Papa to buy one?' asked her brother.
'I don't know, Charlie, if Mamma would like it always,' said Mabel.
'She has such bad headaches, you know.'

Christie's Old Organ

'No,' said Charlie, 'you mustn't think of it, Master Treffy. Let me see, what can we do? Shall *I* take the organ out?'
Old Treffy did not answer: a great struggle was going on in his mind. Could he let anyone but himself touch his dear old organ?

Christie's Old Organ

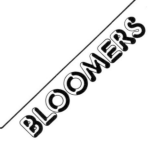

[Sir John Middleton]. . . in winter his private balls were numerous enough for any young lady who was not suffering under the insatiable appetite of fifteen.

Sense and Sensibility

On entering the drawing-room, she found the whole party at loo, and was immediately invited to join them . . .

Pride and Prejudice

BLOOMERS

Patrick Hamilton

*Curtain rises on a room completely darkened
save for the pallid gleam from lamplight in the
street below. Against this are silhouetted the
figures of Granillo and Brandon . . . They are
leaning over the chest, intently, working at
something – exactly what you cannot discern.
Brandon switches on the light at the little table.*

GRANILLO (*at chest*): **Put out that light!
Put out that light!**
Instantly it goes out.
BRANDON (*voice from darkness*): **Steady,
Granno.**
*No reply from the other. Brandon suddenly
lights a match and applies it to his cigarette.
The cigarette glows in the darkness. Pause.*

BRANDON: Feeling yourself, Granno?
No answer.
**BRANDON: Feeling yourself again,
Granno?**
No answer.

Rope (Act one)

BLOOMERS

John Dryden

CHARMIAN: Help, chafe her temples, Iras.
IRAS: Bend, bend her forward quickly.
CHARMIAN: Heaven be praised,
She comes again.

All for Love

Francis Thompson

Her beauty smooth'd earth's furrow'd
    face!
    She gave me tokens three:
A look, a word of her winsome mouth,
    And a wild raspberry.

Daisy

Winthrop Mackworth Praed

She touched the organ; I could stand
    For hours and hours . . .

The Belle of the Ball-room

BLOOMERS

Elizabeth Barrett Browning

No woman was happier in her choice – no
woman – And after above two months of
uninterrupted intercourse, there is still
more and more cause for thankfulness;
– and more and more affection on his side
– He loves me better every day, he says . . .
My health improves still, too.

Letter to Mr H. S. Boyd

BLOOMERS

Henry James

. . . and gradually, when he found his
sensitive organ grateful even for grim
favours, he conferred them with a lighter
hand.

The Portrait of a Lady

Mr Longdon, as he faltered, appeared to
wonder, but emitted a sound of gentleness.
'Yes?'
'Why,' said the stimulated Mitchy, 'do, for
God's sake, just let me have a finger in it.'
Mr Longdon's momentary mystification
was perhaps partly but the natural effect
of constitutional prudence.
'A finger?'
'I mean – let me help.'
'Oh!' breathed the old man thoughtfully
and without meeting his eyes.

The Awkward Age

Mr Longdon, resisting, kept erect with a low gasp that his host only was near enough to catch. This suddenly appeared to confirm an impression gathered by Vanderbank in their contact, a strange sense that his visitor was so agitated as to be trembling in every limb. It brought to his lips a kind of ejaculation,

The Awkward Age

BLOOMERS

I had done Miss Churm at the piano before
– it was an attitude in which she knew how
to take on an absolutely poetic grace.

The Real Thing

'Oh, I can't explain!' cried Roderick
impatiently, returning to his work. 'I've
only one way of expressing my deepest
feelings – it's this.' And he swung his tool.

Roderick Hudson

What an intimacy, what an intensity of
relation, I said to myself, so successful a
process implied! It was of course familiar
enough that when people were so deeply in
love they rubbed off on each other.

The Sacred Fount

BLOOMERS

Both on their feet now, as if ready for the others, they yet – and even a trifle awkwardly – lingered. It might in fact have appeared to a spectator that some climax had come, on the young man's part . . .

The Awkward Age

Next after that slow-coming, slow-going smile of her lover, it was the rusty complexion of his patrimonial marbles that she most prized.

The Last of the Valerii

It was amusing to do Major Monarch's trousers. They *were* the real thing, even if he did come out colossal. It was amusing to do his wife's back hair (it was so mathematically neat) and the particular 'smart' tension of her tight stays. She lent herself especially to positions in which the face was somewhat averted.

The Real Thing

'It's just like Longueville, you know,' Gordon Wright went on; 'he always comes at you from behind; he's so awfully fond of surprises.'

Confidence

BLOOMERS

'You think me a queer fellow already. It's not easy, either, to tell you what I feel, – not easy for so queer a fellow as I to tell you in how many ways he's queer.'

A Passionate Pilgrim

It was the constant theme of his French friends. . . He believed that at bottom he was sorer than they . . . they, however, were perpetually in the breach.

The Princess Casamassima

BLOOMERS

Then she had had her equal consciousness
that, within five minutes, something
between them had – well, she couldn't call
it anything but *come*.

The Wings of the Dove

This time therefore I left the excuses to his
more practised patience, only relieving
myself in response to a direct appeal from
a young lady next whom, in the hall, I
found myself sitting.

The Coxon Fund

She realised at last that she had no
vocation for struggling with her
combinations.

The Portrait of a Lady

BLOOMERS

A. E. Housman

I 'listed at home for a lancer,
  Oh who would not sleep with the brave?

Last Poems

Say, lad, have you things to do?
  Quick then, while your day's at
    prime.
Quick, and if 'tis work for two,
  Here am I, man: now's your time . . .

Ere the wholesome flesh decay,
  And the willing nerve be numb,
And the lips lack breath to say,
  'No, my lad, I cannot come.'

A Shropshire Lad

Frances Hodgson Burnett

'It makes me feel very queer,' he said; 'it makes me feel – queer!' The Earl looked at the boy in silence. It made him feel queer too – queerer than he had ever felt in his whole life. And he felt more queer still when he saw that there was a troubled expression on the small face which was usually so happy . . .

Then he looked up at his grandfather, and there was a wistful shade in his eyes, and they looked very big and soft.

'That other boy,' he said rather tremulously – 'he will have to be your boy now – as I was – won't he?'

'No!' answered the Earl – and he said it so fiercely and loudly that Cedric quite jumped. 'No?' he exclaimed in wonderment. 'Won't he? I thought –'

He stood up from his stool quite suddenly. 'Shall I be your boy, even if I'm not going to be an earl?' And his flushed little face was all alight with eagerness.

How the old Earl did look at him from head to foot, to be sure!

How his great shaggy brows did draw themselves together, and how queerly his

BLOOMERS

deep eyes shone under them – how very queerly!

'My boy!' he said – and, if you'll believe it, his very voice was queer, almost shaky and a little broken and hoarse, not at all what you would expect an earl's voice to be, though he spoke more decidedly and peremptorily even than before – 'yes, you'll be my boy as long as I live; and, by George, sometimes I feel as if you were the only boy I had ever had.'

Cedric's face turned red to the roots of his hair . . .

Little Lord Fauntleroy

41

Dorothy Sayers

'Hang your theories!' said Parker. 'It looks to me as if we shall have to wash out the idea that General Fentiman got his dose in Portman Square.'

The Unpleasantness at the Bellona Club

R. W. Harris

Harley also employed Defoe to write the *Review*, and St John had his own organ in the *Post Boy*.

England in the Eighteenth Century

Alfred Lord Tennyson

Then her cheek was pale and thinner than
 should be for one so young,
And her eye on all my motions with a mute
 observance hung.

Locksley Hall

All my heart
Went forth to embrace him coming
 ere he came.

Oenone

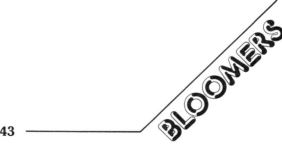

'The curse has come upon me,' cried The Lady of Shalott.

The Lady of Shalott

Angela Thirkell

Mr Grant, really quite glad of an excuse to dismount, offered his cock to Lydia, who immediately flung a leg over it, explaining that she had put on a frock with pleats on purpose.

The Brandons

Robert Louis Stevenson

'Well now, you look here, that was a good lay of yours last night. I don't deny it was a good lay. Some of you pretty handy with a hand-spike end.'

Treasure Island

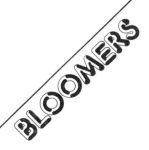

Robert Browning

You brush it, till I grow aware,
  Who wants me, and wide ope I burst.

In a Gondola

Sebald, as we lay,
Rising and falling only with our pants,
Who said 'Let Death come now –
              'tis right to die!'

Pippa Passes

Cowls and twats,
   Monks and nuns, in a cloister's moods,
Adjourn to the oak-stump pantry!

Pippa Passes

A black lynx snarled and pricked a tufted
   ear;
Lust of my blood inflamed his yellow balls.

An Epistle

E. M. Forster

'Stop a minute; let those two people go on,
or I shall have to speak to them. I do detest
conventional intercourse. Nasty! they are
going into the church, too. Oh, the
Britisher abroad!'

A Room with a View

Eustace came too, and knelt quietly
enough between his aunts . . . But when it
was over he at once got up, and began
hunting for something. 'Why! Someone
has cut my whistle in two,' he said.

The Story of a Panic

48

BLOOMERS

Walter Pater

Prince of the school, he had gained an easy
dominion over the old Greek master by the
fascination of his parts.

Marius the Epicurean

Joseph Conrad

Some great men owe most of their
greatness to the ability of detecting in
those they destine for their tools the exact
quality of strength that matters for their
work . . .

Lord Jim

William Johnson Cory

Whate'er is done in this sweet isle,
    There's none that may not lift his horn,
If only lifted with a smile.

Ionica, A Queen's Visit

BLOOMERS

BLOOMERS

Charles Dickens

No public business of any kind could possibly be done at any time, without the acquiescence of the Circumlocution Office. Its finger was in the largest public pie, and in the smallest public tart.

Little Dorrit

I had cherished a profound conviction that her bringing me up by hand gave her no right to bring me up by jerks.

Great Expectations

He had a spectacle case in his hand, which he turned over and over while he was thus in question, with a certain free use of the thumb which is never seen but in a hand accustomed to tools.

Little Dorrit

She touched his organ, and from that bright epoch, even it, the old companion of his happiest hours, incapable as he had thought of elevation, began a new and deified existence.

Martin Chuzzlewit

I deeply appreciate his talent for the organ, notwithstanding that I do not, if I may use the expression, grind myself.

Martin Chuzzlewit

BLOOMERS

Guarini

... for I felt (me thought)
Two fiery balls fly whizzing through my
    liver
And Beauty (a bold thief) cry'd *Stand,
Deliver* ...

> *Il Pastor Fido* translated by
> Sir Richard Fanshawe

George Bubb Dodington

Soon after came the Prince of Wales, and
Prince Edward; and then the Lady
Augusta, all quite undress'd, and took
their stools and sat round the fire with us.

Political Journal

Marcel Proust

'Well!' said the Duchess to me, 'apart from
your balls, can't I be of any use to you?'

Cities of the Plain

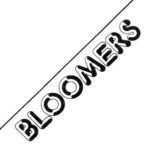

Thomas Hardy

What he had heard was the tear of the ripping tool as it ploughed its way along the sticky parting.

The Woodlanders

It was your way, my dear,
To vanish without a word
When callers, friend or kin
Had left, and I hastened in
To rejoin you, as I inferred.

And when you'd a mind to career
Off anywhere – say to town –
You were all on a sudden gone
Before I had thought thereon,
Or noticed your trunks were down.

Without Ceremony

BLOOMERS

As big as any man could wish to have, and
lined inside, and double-lined in the lower
parts, and an extra piece of stiffening at
the bottom.

Under the Greenwood Tree

BLOOMERS

Henry Vaughan

How brave a prospect is a bright *Back-side*!

Looking Back: Thalia Rediviva

Miscellaneous

FASHIONABLE CHISWICK VILLAGE.
Sunloving Spaniard's Sunny TOP (4th) flr.
MOD. FLAT. LIFT. CENT. HEAT., C.H.W.
inc. ONLY £408 p.a. Set in attractive
communal grnds with trees. (Tenants have
their own small private parts.)

The Sunday Times

Dear Mrs M—,
  It was such fun last night! Thank you so
much for having me, and it was very good
of you to have my partner too. But for you
he would not have come and he did enjoy it
so much.
  Your loving little friend . . .

Letter from a private source

BLOOMERS

Walter de la Mare

Forlornly, silently,
Plays in the evening garden
Myself with me.

Myself

BLOOMERS

C. R. Maturin

From my window I saw them running
through the garden in every direction,
embracing each other, ejaculating,
playing, and counting their beads, with
hands tremulous and eyes uplifted in
ecstacy.

Melmoth the Wanderer

C. S. Lewis

But I remember more dearly autumn
afternoons in bottoms that lay intensely
silent under old and great trees . . .

Surprised by Joy

BLOOMERS

Samuel Johnson

A man who exposes himself when he is intoxicated, has not the art of getting drunk.

Boswell's Life of Johnson

That confidence which presumes to do, by surveying the surface, what labour only can perform, by penetrating the bottom.

Preface to Shakespeare

John Masefield

Go spend you penny, Beauty, when you
  will,
In the grave's darkness let the stamp be
  lost.
The water still will bubble . . .

Lollingdon Downs Sonnet LXVII

BLOOMERS

Dame Ethel Smyth

Having for years had no real intercourse with any one save his wife, he was very shy.

Impressions that Remained

George Eliot

A boy's sheepishness is by no means a sign of over-mastering reverence; and while you are making encouraging advances to him under the idea that he is overwhelmed by a sense of your age and wisdom, ten to one he is thinking you extremely queer.

The Mill on the Floss

BLOOMERS

BLOOMERS

Mrs Glegg had doubtless the glossiest and crispest brown curls in her drawers, as well as curls in various degrees of fuzzy laxness.

The Mill on the Floss

BLOOMERS

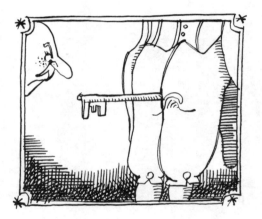

Ouida

(Wilfred Bertram has come back to his
rooms in Piccadilly, to find his trusted
servant Critchett rifling 'a large
Florentine cabinet of tortoise-shell and
brass-work'.)
'How could you open the cabinet? It has a
Bramah lock.'
'And this here's a Bramah pick-lock, sir,'
says Critchett, displaying an elegant little
tool.
'You infernal scoundrel!' repeats Bertram.
'If I did my duty, I should give you to the
police.'

An Altruist

BLOOMERS

Rose Macaulay

Here is a wonderful and delightful thing,
that we should have furnished ourselves
with orifices, with traps that open and
shut, through which to push and pour
alien objects that give us such pleasurable,
such delicious sensations.

Personal Pleasures

R. S. Surtees

Country ladies are not like London ones,
who can take a dinner, an opera, two balls
and an at-home in one and the same night.

Ask Mamma

John Ruskin

Now the time was coming when I began to think about helping princesses by fetching their balls up from the bottom.

Praeterita

BLOOMERS

I am not going to offer – still less urge – marriage now. But I insist on free intercourse – face to face.

Letter to W. Cowper-Temple

William Makepeace Thackeray

The organ 'gins to swell;
    She's coming, she's coming!
My lady comes at last.

At the Church Gate

BLOOMERS

Miss Sedley's new *femme de chambre*
refused to go to bed without a wax candle.

Vanity Fair